Tall Dark & Healing

Tall, Dark & Healing

poems by
Shawn William

Copyright 2025 by Shawn William

All rights reserved. This book or any portion thereof may not be reproduced or used in any manner whatsoever without the express written permission of the publisher except for the use of brief quotations in a book review.

Write About Now Publishing, Texas

www.wanpoetry.com

Print ISBN: 978-0-9906127-6-6

Ebook ISBN: 978-0-9906127-7-3

*This book is dedicated to the memory of
Ethel Marie Gullatt, Wilma Gullatt & Kelly Freeman-Ceballos.*

Poems

First Date Questions 1

Heaven Can Be Hot as Hell 3

First & Last Date Pt. 1 5

Aux Cord Love 6

My World 7

You Just Fit 9

First & Last Date Pt. 2 10

Untitled and Undressed 11

Unofficial Foursome 12

Rainbow 13

Freak Level 14

Black Man's Day 2021 15

Reflection 16

Thank You 17

He's Not Me 18

The Differences (Women) 19

Epiphany	20
Broken & Toxic	21
Black Woman	22
These Hands	23
The Question	25
Eat Pussy for Purposes Bigger than Your Own	26
Civil Rights & Wrongs	28
Give Me Back That, That & That But You Can Keep That Other Shit	29
Heartbreak Anonymous	30
I'll Be Good Without You	31
Temp	32
M.A.S.H. Unit	34
Things I Miss	35
Our Future Daughter	36
Someone's Daughter Is Going To Be Happy	37
Sometimes	38
Love Poet	39

Women Watcher/Thigh Meat Season 41

Seen 43

Love, Cheesecake Factory & Keke 45

With All of This Womanizing That I Do What Should I Tell My Son? ....
.... 46

Accountability 48

Serial Monogamist 50

What Does My Healing Look Like? 52

A Letter to My Next Woman 54

First Date Questions

Are you married?
Do you have a boyfriend?
Do you have a girlfriend?
Does anyone in North America or any of the other 6 continents think you are their girlfriend?
Have you ever stabbed anyone?
Where?
Did they die?
Do you like your tacos corn or flour shell?
That's a trick question because corn shell tacos are the ONLY type of tacos you should eat.
Are your car tires bald?
Is the check engine light on?
How long has the check engine light been on?
Do you have any children?
How many?
Do any of them have silver capped teeth?
Why did you give them so much juice?
Have you ever slept with any NBA, NFL, NBL, players that I'd root for, or Drake?
Do you think R. Kelly is guilty?

Do you have a relationship with your father?

Have you ever had a healthy relationship with a man that has lasted more than a year?

If your best friend disrespected me would you let it slide or check them?

Do you love yourself?

What does loving yourself look like?

Heaven Can Be Hot as Hell

It was passionate–intense.
No other words in the world could explain
what I was feeling. It's like this
might be the last time
we see each other because this crazy
world is collapsing around us and you,
my Angel, I know that you're going to heaven.

But me?

Well my past sins might not get me through
those pearly gates. So for me you slid to the side
your "secrets" and let me taste your pearly gates.

That night we went from early to late. To say
that we just had sex is so disrespectful
for what happened. Almost like saying you're just a woman.

Sweat mixing with your sugar walls, we climbed mountains
and brought down walls put up to protect our hearts
from past relationships.

Both of us too afraid of those 3 words,
but passion like that could not be faked.

You felt my passion & love
on my down stroke, and I felt you inside
& out, hugging me tight. Shit, woman you sweated
out my hair that night. From 0-60 I went
from 360 brush waves to having buckshots.
You allowed me to grab your hair
as I kissed the small of your back
as you thanked me for every stiff back shot.

Nails scratched my back to keep track
& scores every time I hit that spot.
And when I came it was my white flag
letting you know that I surrender.

Do you remember that night?
It was so fucking hot,
sins mixed with confessions.

If being perfect is impossible, then that night we were close
to seeing perfection, like me being close to this mic,
like you being close to saying,
"I want you forever in my life."

So I thank you my Angel for allowing this 6'5 sinner
to get a glimpse of heaven in your eyes,
between your thighs & in your heart
that night.

First & Last Date Pt. 1

She asked for her steak well done
I asked for separate checks

Aux Cord Love

When I got in her car
& she played "What We Do" by Freeway
I was impressed
When she said his lines word for word
Without mumble, stutter, or fumble
I immediately pulled out my phone
Text my brothers, "She's the one"
Changed my relationship status
Started looking online for engagement rings
Princess, radiant, or marquise cut
Whatever she wants, I'm getting
3 months' salary is well worth it because any woman
That can rap
One of my favorite songs from The R.O.C.
Deserves one
Aux Cord Love

My World

I want us to travel the world together & make memories
Have the pleasure of giving you multiples with a fistful of your hair
While bending you over balconies overlooking a world
That is in so much need of our love
You are the woman of my dreams
That I am so happy to wake up to
Would be perfectly ok
Laying in the bed with you being lazy
All day
But you motivate me to get up
Keep creating, be great
Not to worry
Because with a kiss you promise
That what I'm craving right now will be there when I get back home
You are home
Fully furnished
A meal that nourishes
I can live a lifetime in between your legs & thoughts
The thought of losing you scares me just
As much as my son growing up in this ugly cold cruel world

You have met my son, my mother, my father
And more importantly
I've allowed you to meet me

All of me
Open & honest
Vulnerable & flawed
Licking away the salt
 That covered my wounds
Keloid my scars

You're my Venus, I'm your Mars
Let us rule together
Follow my lead
I will trust your judgement
I provide
You procreate
We'll prosper
Making beautiful black babies
That will break generational curses
While creating generational wealth
WE YOU ME US

I want us to travel the world together & make memories
Have the pleasure of giving you multiples with a fist full of your hair
While bending you over balconies overlooking a world
That is in so much need of our love

You Just Fit

You fit perfectly around my erection
Long limbs lock on like you want me to stay awhile
The way that you yell "Fuck" out loud
Sounds like you dropped something
Maybe it was your guard
The past
Hints that you want this to be more
Than a stop by
I warned you that this mouth does more
Than just poems

First & Last Date Pt. 2

Her- "I really don't like Jodeci"
Me- "Waiter can I get the check & to-go boxes please?"

Untitled and Undressed

"Put on this blindfold"
Covered her ears with my headphones
Laid her down
Opened her legs
Slowly

Trust must be established first

I plug the headphones into my phone
Play track 12 on D'Angelo's second album
And give her head
For 7 minutes & 10 seconds

She came in my mouth 2 times
And I enjoyed every drop
Of her "Thank you"

Sometimes unnecessary
Sounds & sights can distract you
From a good thing

Unofficial Foursome

Have you ever had a threesome
With two bad ass women
Their legs longer than your credit report
In a penthouse suite
With a view overlooking
A world that's ready to be fucked
Harder than these two beautiful
Women in your bed
And all you keep thinking about is the
Problematic text that your ex sent you 16 hours & 36 minutes ago?
No?
Just me?
Damn

Rainbow

The only reason why I do this poetry shit
Is to one day be famous
Enough to take a sundress & Jordan 1's wearing Tracee Ellis-Ross
Out on a picnic
Eat lemon pepper wings,
Seasoned fries, drink coconut mojitos
Listen to Frankie Beverly & Maze Greatest Hits
As I lotion those
Long lovely legs

Freak Level

"How freaky are you?"

"Freakier than Prince having a 'menage with Nicki Minaj & Lil' Kim off 3 perks & a pint of bumpy faced gin while listening to Rick James records scratched backwards"

"But, don't play with my booty"

Black Man's Day 2021

I want you to hold me I want to lay my head
On your lap—be vulnerable
Cry ten years of tears into your denim
Confess all the pains & demons
That I hold inside tighter than Aries grudges
Without judgment or advice. Be there.

Listen

These streets want to kill me
Corporate America won't let me live
Family trauma catching up
And depression constantly calling from blocked numbers

I don't know if I'm writing suicide letters or vulnerability poems
But I'm realizing that they're becoming Signature pieces
I just want you to hold me
Lay my head on your lap—be vulnerable
Cry ten years of tears into your denim While confessing all the pains & demons
That I hold inside tighter than Aries grudges
But I remember you telling me the other day,
"These dudes be acting too emotional these days,
I'm glad that you ain't one of those sensitive Niggas."

Reflection

The other day our son
Walked into the kitchen,
Looking for familiar,
Turned around looking at me
With the same facial expression
That you make &
It made me miss you all over again

Thank You

For sacrificing your body
To provide me the greatest gift of all

For surviving cancer
To give birth to a Cancer
For creating someone
Who means everything

My first reflection
A mixture of us & better times
Thank You

He's Not Me

He could never make you laugh like I could…or cry either.
I guess that's why we're not together?

The Differences (Women)

When a woman gets out of a relationship her best friend is informed about it. By text message or carrier pigeon, it's beautiful, unifying, breathtaking. Said best friend walks to the dresser, pulls out a flare gun, goes to the balcony & shoots it into the sky as an explosion goes into the air saying SOS which stands for "Save our sista" as women from across the country jump in Hondas, Toyotas, & Jettas on a half a tank of gas with self-help books, wine, & weed brownies to come to their girl's time of need. Lauryn Hill songs are played (a lot). Beyoncé's videos are watched (a lot). Trips to Jamaica & Cancun are planned and fitness boot camp memberships go up. As beautiful bodies slim down to fit into tight & sleek form fitting "Fuck em girl" dresses. "Fuck em girl" is said by her best friend (a lot) every time the girlfriend tries to get off track. Example:
Her- "I wonder if he misses me?"
BFF- "Fuck em girl!"
Her- "Should I reply to this text?"
BFF- "Fuck em girl!"
Her- "I met this new guy who looks good what should I do?"
BFF- "You should FUCK HIM GIRL"
As her social media stories & posts reflect the times "NEW YEAR, NEW ME" & "I CAN DO BAD BY MY DAMN SELF"
As the healing process to mend her broken heart begins

Epiphany

Today I realized that your ring payments lasted longer than our marriage.

Broken & Toxic

After we broke up
I slept with every woman that
You accused me of cheating on you with
Hoped their moans from firm back shots
Were earshots away
So that you can hear
The pitiful, pettiness of my pain

Black Woman

A good woman can have your back but a good Black woman can be your spine.

These Hands

"There's a lot you can learn from a man by the size of his hands & length of his fingers" – said to me by a flirtatious woman at Happy Hour
I'm not afraid to get my hands dirty
But when touching you, hands & nails must be clean & manicured
With these hands, man, I cure ailments
Rub out knots
Find spots you never knew existed
With pinpoint precision that
Make Fenty's moist
While you niggas trick off, buying them
Expensive bags & red bottoms
I bag them by removing heels & rub the red bottoms of their feet
It's the very least
That I could do for
Her standing up for us Black men
Plus I'm a pleaser
Teaser
There's something about putting pressure with your thumb
Pushing up to the toes
That loosens push up bras
Working & caressing Ankles
Calves
Knees
Hips

Magically & miraculously
Opens the valley of thighs
To view the fountain of youth
Now an amateur would pull his manhood out,
Be selfish & start stroking
A pro would put his face in & let juices
Moisten his beard
Me? I let my fingers finish the job it started
Rubbing around
Up & down Finger
In Out
Take it out &
Then put it in my mouth
Look at her & say "come closer"
With the same index finger
So she can get a taste of her
Sharing the juice box like poor kids
At lunch break
Stand her vertically to continue
We dirty dance
Simulating the samba I lead, she follows
I sip
She swallows
Legs buckle
Suck the bottom of your lip
Continuing to moisten your clit
As my finger touches places
That the last niggas that you fucked with
Couldn't reach with his dick
Shit
You're dealing with a man
Who is very good with his hands hands on whatever
You give consent to touch
I will
Trust me love
I will

The Question

Question
Have you ever sat on the shoulders of a giant?
Touched the ceiling while being tasted
Laid on a dining room table, legs wide open
In front of a starving man & the only thing that can nourish his body is you?
There is nothing more beautiful than a queen exploding on king size Bed sheets turning satin into slip-n-slides
The euphoria in her eyes as pleasure pulsates
Pure
Sweet
Unadulterated decadence
Turning creamy wet pools
Deep enough to dive in So I dive in head first
Because you look like you like head first

Black beards mop up wet floors I inhale intimacy
You exhale ecstasy
Tongue kissing pearl tongues
Have you losing your mind & religion
My mission is to curve your toes like you've been curving niggas all week
Because right now you're feeling me
All of me

Eat Pussy for Purposes Bigger than Your Own

Baby I don't eat pussy to
Get head back
I eat pussy because I love eating pussy
Love seeing you squirt & squirm
Knowing that when it's time
To vote between me & the next
nigga that I will win the electoral votes
In the states of Florida, California, Georgia & Texas

I eat pussy so well you'd
Think that I was cheating on you
It feels like I'm apologizing for something major
Make you want to stop me
Ask for my phone & password
So you can find out what
Bitch I've been texting behind your back

Make exes check on me
Shake your leg so hard
That when it kicks the bottom bed board
It sounds like the thumping noise Al Green made
Right before the electric guitar strummed on the song

"Love & Happiness"

I am a grown ass man
That knows how to pleasure
A grown ass woman
Don't need directions on how to find shit
Not every woman deserves this
But for the ones who do I do it well & often

Civil Rights & Wrongs

...f**k the revolution
We should make passionate love
Like when Malcolm met Betty after coming back from Mecca
Let's cheat on each other with each other.
Be hos signing in with fake names at random hotels
You can be Ruby & I'll be Ossie
Or even Whitney & Bobby
As long as we continue to touch & satisfy our bodies

Give Me Back That, That & That But You Can Keep That Other Shit

I want my hoodie, basketball shorts, & my beanie back,
But you can keep my heart
That thing gets me into too much trouble.

Heartbreak Anonymous

Women think that I buy them shoes to spoil them
I buy shoes to replace the old ones that have stains
From the eggshells I make them walk on
I told you that I wasn't a picnic
Your background check should've included my breakups
I am a vampire who writes "I'm sorry" notes in cursive in front mirrors unable to see my wrongs or reflections so if I can't see me, how in the hell do you think I can see you & I together?

Baby this has nothing to do with the extra weight that you put on carrying my burdens, I was just waiting for the right time to break your heart which is normally around the time you are ready to give your heart to me and after all these years of hurting women, you'd think I'd be praying for forgiveness but I was just waiting for my next prey.

She's probably that fine ass individual who hasn't had her father in her life long enough to warn her about a man like me.
Hi, you don't need to know my name because we won't be together long enough for you to curse it.

I'll Be Good Without You

My biological mother abandoned me at birth
Adopted mother put me out the house at 16 Nana died of cancer at 19
Every important woman in my life left me & I survived
I say all that to ask you
What makes you think
That I can't handle you leaving?

Temp

You were time spent
Trauma was the only thing
We had in common
We only met after 10pm
To do one thing
And we did that "one thing" well
We never ate at each other's favorite restaurants
Never walked the lake
This was all during a global pandemic
So I made sure that I kept my heart
6 ft away from you because
Love is a virus that I'm not willing to catch
From you
I was not interested in meeting your child
You would never meet mine
If we saw each other in traffic
Play your position
Keep it pushing
And pay me no mind
This is not a "situation-ship"
Just house calls
From "Doctor feel good"
A "give & go"
From a playa that's nice

With the 'rock'
Temp job
Seasonal
No chance of going permanent
No benefits
You could be let go at any time
By a phone call or text
Not even a face to face
No nameplate
No pictures
And definitely no title
Our misery was our company
And for 6 weeks
Business was good
"Thank you for all your hard work but I must inform you that your services are no longer needed.
I have hired a full-time replacement"

M.A.S.H. Unit

Toxic orgasms are amazing but also problematic
When you cried
I knew those tears weren't for me
I was perfectly fine with that
My mind was elsewhere too
We talk about our exes
Then fuck each other
Like they fucked us over
We shared scars & war stories
Doing our best patch up jobs
There were times that you felt like my therapist & sex slave
Our names didn't matter
We barely went outside the house

We just gave each other what we needed and then went on with our lives
We shouldn't build relationships on past trauma but we did.

Things I Miss

The thing that I miss
The most is your lips
The way
You made deceptions
Sound so good
Taste like truth
Feel like confirmation
You had an uncanny way
Of lying to my face
With so much passion & conviction I believed
Every sentence
Becoming a prisoner
Of the moment.

Our Future Daughter

Our daughter's name will be "Naomi"
She will be a beautiful chocolate brown dynamo with a 1000 watt smile
Charming like her father
Intelligent like her mother
Tall like the both of us
Fluent in 4 languages
English, French, Italian, & Code Switch
Revolutionary & Ratchet
Nerdy & Thuglife
Know how to shoot a glock & a jump shot
Graduate from Spellman
Grad school at Howard
Pledge Black Girl Magic
And be walked down the aisle by a crying man

Someone's Daughter Is Going To Be Happy

She's not going to worry about wearing heels & towering over her man
She's going to get my hoodie, basketball shorts, colorful socks, & the food on my plate since mine "tastes better" plus she's worth it.

I will be the big spoon & lose arm circulation for love
Massage her feet, booty, & scalp
Plus listen to her work stories & adlib with
"You right" or "That b**** is crazy"
Someone's daughter is about to get all these hugs, silliness, & grammatically correct text messages because I know that she hates typos
Someone's daughter is going to get the best of me constantly, consistently & be loved unconditionally. Hand holding, long walks & baecations, passports stamped up

So if you're out there, because I know that you're out there, waiting to be adored by a man that has so much love to give, rolling eyes & laughing so hard at corny "Dad jokes" that your abs hurt I know that you're scared
I know that you've been down this road before with dudes that were "dusty" & "ashy, "but try again.
"Stop playing, you know you like me"
Love,
Someone's Son

Sometimes

Burning bridges with people
Is necessary because some paths
Should never be traveled again

Love Poet

My artistry is at its best
When I'm heartbroken
When most men
Close themselves off to the world
Too afraid to share their pain
I open up my notebook & create
I used to hate every woman
For how they made me feel
But now I thank them
Embrace the pain
More than I embraced
Their wants & needs
My favorite sayings are "Then go!"
&
"This isn't working"
Quick to quit
The job than put in the full-time hours
Why continue to water flowers
When they're bound to die anyway
Just buy new ones
Every time it's spring time
You always see me with a new one
Sprung
Nose wide open like legs

But I'm not a misogynist
I'm a masochist
Kiss the girls & make them cry
My "I love yous" sound just like my "goodbyes"
I take pleasure in pain and suffering
For my heart
For my love
For my son
And my art
It's my cross to bear
And didn't
Jesus suffer on his cross
For our sins?
My sin is that I constantly confuse loyalty with love
Attract shorter women with my height
Knowing that they'll never reach my
High expectations.

Woman Watcher/Thigh Meat Season

Sitting on the grass at Lake Merritt

Black & magenta maxi dress
Showing your back out
& your backyard
Slit revealing just enough 'thigh meat'
To let people know them morning
Workouts are working
Out just fine

Ankle bracelet on left leg
Touching the straps of your Stuart
Weitzman sandal
Toes pedicured, polished &
Detailed like your 4 door car parked on
The side street off Grand Ave
Next to Round Table
Because meter maids be tripping

You look "Summertime Fine"
So "fine" that I'd hike those
Stairs with shoes
Two sizes too small
Because you definitely are a

Step up

You wear Perlier Shea Butter huh?
Like Tacos & Tequila?
Got an inbox full of DMs
From a bunch of "DMs" (Don't Matters)
Boys who don't know the correct use of "Their", "There", & "They're"
So you leave them on read because
What you're not gon' do is stress
Those strong edges of yours out
Over no mere mortal when you are a goddess

Got-Damn you're "Summertime fine"
And you don't need any man to tell you this
This makes you even more fine
More attractive
Look like my future

I want us to live in the present
But instead I let you pass
Because sometimes beauty Just needs to be witnessed
And not bothered

Seen

You love me
Not the thought of me
Not the height of me
The poems
The charisma or persona
But me
You don't give a damn about the claps or cheers
You care about my fears
My health
My son
Wanting to be my moon
My future with or without you
You ask about my father
Want me to make peace with my mother
You pray for me
Pray with me Stayed with me
You cried for me
When I wouldn't
Couldn't
You love me
Not the idea of me
But me
The real me
The me I refused to see

Or let others see
You believe in me
When I didn't believe in me
You see me for who I am
Beautiful
Strong when weak
Hurting when silent
Angry when quiet
And for that
I will always love you

Love, Cheesecake Factory & Keke

You're the only woman that I ever thought
About going back to
Daydreams of us walking
Oceanside
In the Summer
Skipping work because PTO days were made
For these moments
I remember the first time
That I said those 3 words
We were at the Cheesecake Factory
Overlooking the city
When the server who already complimented
My shoes earlier
Laughed at my joke a little too healthily
You said & I quote
"Keke, could you see if our food is ready please?"
The server seemed confused on who
You were talking to & said "My name is Jennifer"
Where you replied "You'd think your name was Keke
The way you were Keke'n with my man"
That shit was so black girl hard I had
To look you in the eyes & say "I love you"
And I never stopped.

With All of This Womanizing That I Do What Should I Tell My Son?

I'm working on myself
It's often childish
Manipulating
Borderline
Narcissistic

I never cheated on your mother
With another woman
But I did cheat her from
A lot of days of happiness

I have no excuse for my behavior
Can't blame it on watching your
Grandfather
Because he is the best example of
How a man should love a woman correctly

I have the PDA correct
It's just the internal affairs that I need to get in order
I'm getting better I'm slowing down
3 decades of erasing misogyny
Without a ring on my finger is a tough task

That I'm working on daily
I'm addicted to the desire
A flirtatious junky
I apologize for using you
When going grocery shopping
Or social media posting

Your purpose in this world is much
More than being my wingman
So for you not to follow in my footsteps
I have to go down a better path

Accountability

"I need to sit down
& Love myself more"

Things that brothas
Don't do or say enough
I'm a beautiful black man
Tall, charming, & charismatic
But also broken beyond belief
That attracts the same
There are 3 decades
Of sexism & misogyny
That needs therapy
Just because I don't call a woman "bitch"
Doesn't mean that I don't at times treat them as such
My superpowers are
That I can passionately fuck a woman
Without loving her
Become your best friend
& then break up with you leaving you
Emotionally bankrupt

These aren't my intentions
It's these women in my DMs & Twitter mentions that keep begging
For my atte…….

Nah, that shit was too rhymey
Plus it's not taking accountability
For my act (Shawn's)

I'm a 3rd generation womanizer
Trying to break generational curses
Daily because my son deserves better

I'm cheap with women who deserve more
And trick on women who are only out to trick me

I need to sit my ass down
Address my childhood traumas
Stay off IG
And focus on myself
Because my "body count" is starting
To catch up with my "followers"

Serial Monogamist

When we broke up I cried
When we broke up I went on a date later on that night
When we broke up I had the worst performance ever
When we broke up I had my best performance ever
When we broke up I didn't even know that I was in a relationship
When we broke up I stopped going to the Cheesecake Factory in San Francisco
When we broke up I went to NBA All-Star Weekend and acted like a whole whore
When we broke up I put a stripper through community college
When we broke up you tried to keep my class ring & letterman's jacket but my girl cousins wasn't having that & met you at the bus stop with Vaseline on their face
When we broke up I was sad that I never met your father
When we broke up I was glad that you never met my son
When we broke up I blocked your number & unfollowed you on IG
When we broke up I asked Mrs. Sanchez if I could move my seat away from yo ass
When we broke up I told myself "Don't get back with this crazy ass woman"
Then we broke up 2 months later so look who's the crazy one.
I am a serial Monogamist, a lover of love. I love hard & often.
Let's keep it a bean, my heart's like Kobe Bean Bryant on the wing of every 4th quarter, I will always take the shot without a care,

unconsciously, if I miss I'll shoot again, I will never pass because love to me is the ultimate victory. Other 'players' talk shit on the sidelines but never get 'chips', I approach love with a chip on my shoulder. Never regret, every love is a lesson & every lover was a blessing. If I ever told a woman "I love you" she knew I meant it. It might have been too much for her or not enough for her but she still knew.
She knew.

What Does My Healing Look Like?

A steak dinner in downtown Denver
Langston's laugher followed by "I love you Daddy"

Talking to Tone or Bev without bringing her name up once

A flight out of SFO, emergency row exit seat, headphones & hoodie on, sipping cran-apple juice with a beautiful flight attendant asking me what am I working on

Sip & Paint in Sacramento Meditation mornings
Consistent skincare regiments & water consumption
A pedicure in Hawaii
Retail Therapy at the Express for Men Outlet
Healthy conversations with my child's mother in front of our child
Giving her Mother's Day gifts in front of our child
Being proud of saying "Our child"
Healing looks like:
Weight loss Muscle gain
Healthy beard
Loving every grey & wrinkle
Fishing on Tuesdays
Bike riding on Wednesdays
Walking the Lake on Thursdays
Watching old movies on Fridays

It's being able to see you on IG & be happy for your new man

It's being able to see you on IG & not give two fucks about your new man
It's replying to your text
It's not replying to your text
Deleting your number
Deleting old photos
Deleting old videos (especially THOSE videos)
Leaving you on "Unread"
Being unbothered
Being Unapologetic
Realizing that I was often underappreciated but there's a woman waiting for all this love & not afraid to love me back
Healing looks like saying "I apologize" without expecting sex or an apology back.
Healing looks like this book.

A Letter to My Next Woman

I prayed for you
Started eating healthy
Drinking more water
Getting my credit stronger
Went back to therapy to tackle family issues & trauma
So if we get into an argument it's just us having an argument
Not the ghost of my mother or exes

My exes, have been forgiven, blocked or told about you
I "Cc'd every girl that I see, see'd round town"
There will be no doubling back or circling the block
I've studied my part of why they didn't work
Worked on myself
Learned lessons to prepare me for what I want and need when dating you

You, you will get the best of me
Feel safe around me
Be heard
Supported
Needed
And loved

Let those raggedy podcasts argue about "50/50 splits" and what they bring to the table

I want to create 100% equity in a house
Business
So generational wealth can be spread throughout our blended family
Your child is now my child
My child now yours
Neither needing a new mommy or daddy
Just a beautiful view of someone properly loving their mommy & daddy

Woman I'm ready to blow your back out
Be your soulmade who steals your soul
Takes your breath away
Our love making will touch every love language

Physical touch
Affirmations
Gift giving
Quality time
Acts of kindness

I promise you, whoever was before me ain't me

I need you to be over him
Be comfortable with who you are
Love yourself
Pilates is cool, but please exercise patience
Take accountability
Because we are each other's gifts not adversaries

There's so much love and kindness inside of me ready to be unlocked by
The right woman
My fists are scratched and scared from fighting demons and guarding my heart

Woman I prayed for yoou

Asked god to deliver you
To kiss every freckle and stretch mark
Turning imperfections perfect

But until that day comes
Keep healing
Keep reading those self care books
Put "Find love" on your vision board
Love yourself and that beautiful child of ours
Until our paths finally cross
Don't let your single friends talk about how dirty these dating streets are
Look across those streets, to the neighborhood park, there you'll see me
By the swings
Waiting
Ready
Healed

Dedication and Acknowledgements

First & foremost I'd like to thank my God & Savior for forever looking over me while providing this path to travel & create on. To my family who have stood by me through all the ups and downs. To my brotha from another mother Tone, to your mother who made herself my mother when mine passed away Mama Pam. To every spoken word venue for allowing me safe spaces to elevate my gift. To all my followers & supporters who have rode this journey with me. Thanks Amir for offering this opportunity to be published through Write About Now. Thanks to Chibbi & the entire WAN family for making this book a reality.

This book is dedicated to every woman who I provide space to occupy my heart. I appreciated & learned from every experience. Many of you poured into me but unfortunately when you have chemistry, sometimes it can turn into toxins. If I ever told you, "I love you", I meant it; if you ever replied "I love you", then I received it. "I love, love" and will forever strive to get it, unconditionally without trauma or guilt.

To my Son Langston, when you are old enough to read this understand that loving hard is hard, but it's the only way & if you've done all that you could & love walks away, let it go but never let go of love.

Love,
Shawn

Shawn William is a Grammy Nominated spoken word artist, published author, storyteller & father hailing from Oakland, California. For over 20 years of dedication & hard work his writing & performance skills have allowed him to performed at the Apollo Theatre, Radio City Music Hall, The Essence Festival, feature on The Arsenio Hall Show and Verses and Flow, while also being one of 5 artist selected to have a residency at The Kennedy Center.

Other Books from Write About Now Publishing

Mexican Dinosaur by C.L. "Rooster" Martinez

We All Make it Out in the End by Lacey Roop

Golden Brown Skin by S.C. Says

OTRO/PATRIA by M.R. "Chibbi" Orduña

Going Down Singing by Kevin Burke

They Rewrote Themselves Legendary by Ronnie K. Stephnes

Universe in the Key of Matryoshka by Ronnie K. Stephens

Rebel Hearts & Restless Ghosts by William James

And then Came the Flood by Lacey Roop

www.ingramcontent.com/pod-product-compliance
Lightning Source LLC
Chambersburg PA
CBHW051603010526
44118CB00023B/2802